SCIENCE EXPLORER

EROSION

SUPER COOL
SCIENCE
EXPERIMENTS:
EROSION

by Ariel Kazunas and Charnan Simon

CHERRY LAKE PUBLISHING • ANN ARBOR, MICHIGAN

Published in the United States of America by
Cherry Lake Publishing
Ann Arbor, Michigan
www.cherrylakepublishing.com

Content Editor: Robert Wolffe, EdD,
Professor of Teacher Education,
Bradley University, Peoria, Illinois

Book design and illustration: The Design Lab

Grateful acknowledgment to Deborah Simon, Department of Chemistry,
Whitman College

Photo Credits: Cover and page 1, ©Patricia Hofmeester, used under
license from Shutterstock, Inc.; page 5, ©Hallgerd, used under license
from Shutterstock, Inc.; page 7, ©Gelpi/Dreamstime.com; page 9,
©Naffarts/Dreamstime.com; page 13, ©iStockphoto.com/jamievanbuskirk;
page 17, ©Martinmark/Dreamstime.com; page 21, ©Barsik/Dreamstime.
com; page 25, ©paul prescott, used under license from Shutterstock, Inc.

Library of Congress Cataloging-in-Publication Data
Kazunas, Ariel.
  Super cool science experiments: Erosion / by Ariel Kazunas and
Charnan Simon.
      p. cm.—(Science explorer)
  Includes bibliographical references and index.
  ISBN-13: 978-1-60279-525-9   ISBN-10: 1-60279-525-8 (lib. bdg.)
  ISBN-13: 978-1-60279-603-4   ISBN-10: 1-60279-603-3 (pbk.)
  1. Erosion—Experiments—Juvenile literature. I. Simon, Charnan.
II. Title. III. Title: Erosion. IV. Series.
  QE576.K39 2010
  551.3'02078—dc22   2009009356

Cherry Lake Publishing would like to acknowledge the work
of The Partnership for 21st Century Skills. Please visit
www.21stcenturyskills.org for more information.

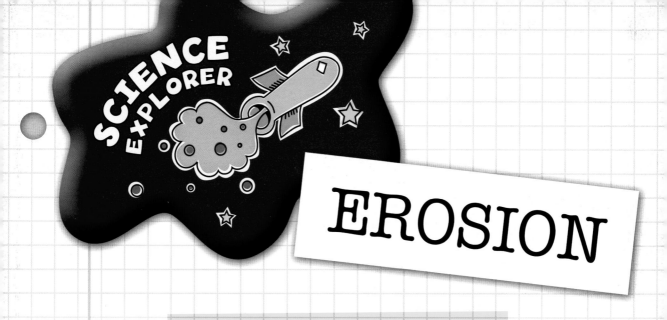

EROSION

TABLE OF CONTENTS

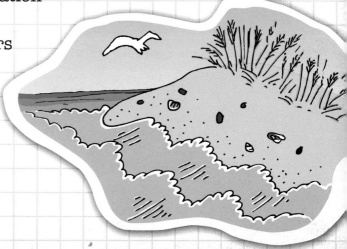

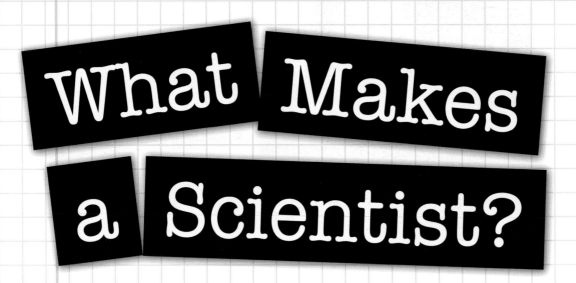

What Makes a Scientist?

Have you ever thought about what it takes to be a scientist? Could you be one? Most scientists aren't that different from anyone else. When they have questions, for example, they want to find answers. Scientists aren't happy with only looking things up in a book, though. They also like to do experiments to test what they think the answer will be. Did you know you can do the same thing, using materials you have at home? In this book, we'll learn how scientists think as we experiment with erosion. We'll even learn how to design our own experiments!

Scientists enjoy asking questions and finding the answers.

First Things First

Have you ever taken a close look at rocks?

Scientists learn by studying something very carefully. For example, geologists are scientists who study erosion. They notice that everything, from rocks to mountains, wears down over time. They understand that Earth's materials get moved from place to place. They do experiments to understand how and why.

Good scientists take notes on everything they discover. They write down their observations. Sometimes those observations lead scientists to ask new questions. With new questions in mind, they design experiments to find the answers.

When scientists design experiments, they must think very clearly. The way they think about problems is often called the scientific method. What is the scientific method? It's a step-by-step way of finding answers to specific questions. The steps don't always follow the same pattern. Sometimes scientists change their minds. The process often works something like this:

Scientific method

- **Step One:** A scientist gathers the facts and makes observations about one particular thing.
- **Step Two:** The scientist comes up with a question that is not answered by all the observations and facts.
- **Step Three:** The scientist creates a hypothesis. This is a statement of what the scientist thinks is probably the answer to the question.
- **Step Four:** The scientist tests the hypothesis. He or she designs an experiment to see whether the hypothesis is correct. The scientist does the experiment and writes down what happens.
- **Step Five:** The scientist draws a conclusion based on how the experiment turned out. The conclusion might be that the hypothesis is

correct. Sometimes, though, the hypothesis is not correct. In that case, the scientist might develop a new hypothesis and another experiment.

In the following experiments, we'll see the scientific method in action. We'll gather some facts and observations about erosion. And for each experiment, we'll develop a question and a hypothesis. Next, we'll do an actual experiment to see if our hypothesis is correct. By the end of the experiment, we should know something new about erosion. Scientists, are you ready? Then let's get started!

Get ready to think like a scientist!

Experiment #1

Worn by Weathering—Rusting Away

Erosion is the process by which Earth's materials are worn and carried away. An important part of this process is weathering. Weathering is the wearing down of rocks and minerals into smaller pieces that are easier to move. If the atoms and molecules of these materials are actually changed into new ones as this happens, we call it chemical weathering. Mechanical weathering happens if a physical force such as wind breaks the materials apart. The atoms and molecules are left unchanged. Biological weathering results if plants and animals are responsible for wearing down or changing the materials.

Have you ever seen objects—a car in the rain, a bridge over water, even a rock in a moist area—with red spots, or rust, all over them? What's going on here? Is this a type of weathering? Could water have something to do with the change in these objects? And does the type of water—salt water or freshwater—make a difference? Let's do an experiment to find out! Come up with a hypothesis about water and rust. Here is one possibility: **An object will rust more quickly if it is wet than if it is dry.**

Have you ever walked on a sidewalk that was cracked or made uneven by tree roots? This is just one example of biological weathering. Roots can work their way through cracks in rock. The cracks eventually split open, creating smaller rock pieces.

Here's some rust on a metal watering can.

Here's what you'll need:

- 3 shallow dishes that are the same size
- 3 pieces of steel wool
- Rubber cleaning gloves
- A tablespoon
- Water
- Salt
- Tape
- Marker

Do you have everything? Then let's get started!

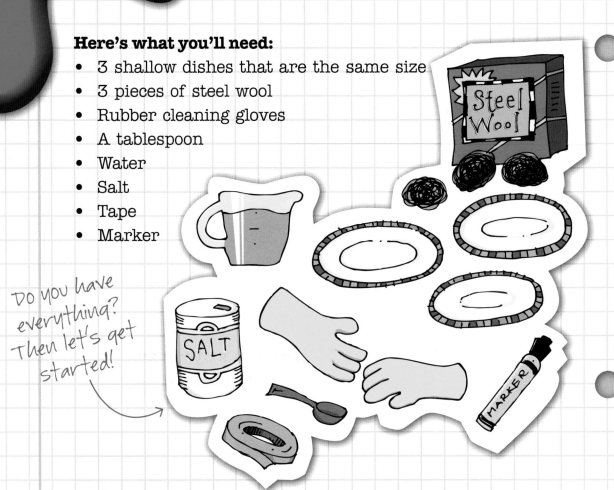

Instructions:

1. Use a piece of tape and marker to label the first dish "Water," the second dish "Salt Water," and the third dish "Dry."
2. Place 1 piece of steel wool that is about the size of a golf ball in each dish. Use gloves when handling steel wool because you could get splinters. Ouch!
3. Fill the "Water" and "Salt Water" dishes halfway with water.

4. Sprinkle 1 tablespoon of salt over the steel wool in the "Salt Water" dish.
5. The "Dry" dish should only have the piece of steel wool in it (no water).
6. Let the dishes sit for 7 days. Observe them every day. Record the date and time you do so. Write down how the steel wool changes each day.
7. On Day 7, put on the gloves and take the pieces of steel wool out of their dishes.
8. Hold the steel wool that was in the salt water. Try to pull it apart. Rub it between your fingers.
9. Do the same with the freshwater and dry samples.
10. Write down your observations as you handle each sample. Pay attention to how each sample reacts.

Be sure to write down what you see each day.

Conclusion:

Which piece looks the most different after 7 days? Does it crumble easily when handled? Do the wet pieces look very different from the dry piece? Was your hypothesis correct?

Water contains oxygen. Oxidation is the process in which oxygen combines with other things. When oxygen reacts with iron, something called iron oxide forms. Most people call this rust. Can you guess why we used steel wool for this experiment? Steel is made from iron.

Moisture helps speed up the rusting process. Salt speeds up the rusting of iron, too. The rust makes the steel wool weaker. Does this help explain your findings? You've just demonstrated an example of chemical weathering.

In nature, objects don't always have to sit in water to get rusty. Moist air can do the same thing. Some rocks contain iron. When moist air reacts with this iron, rust forms on the rock. It eventually erodes away like the crumbly wool in your experiment.

Experiment #2

Worn by Weathering— Freeze and Thaw

Have you ever wondered why roads get potholes? You may have noticed that potholes collect water easily. Do you live someplace where it gets cold during winter? You may have also noticed that the water in those potholes can freeze, thaw, and freeze again all winter long.

Look out for potholes!

Could weathering be the culprit behind potholes? Come up with a hypothesis. Here is one option: **The repeated freezing and thawing of water in the cracks of cement or rocks can break those materials apart.**

Here's what you'll need:
- 2 empty 1-pint (0.5 liter) milk cartons, with the tops cut off
- 2–3 cups of white flour
- 1–2 cups of warm water
- Bowl
- Spoon
- Small balloon
- Freezer

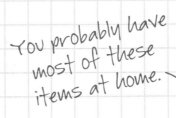
You probably have most of these items at home.

Experiment #3

Eaten by Erosion—Blown Bare

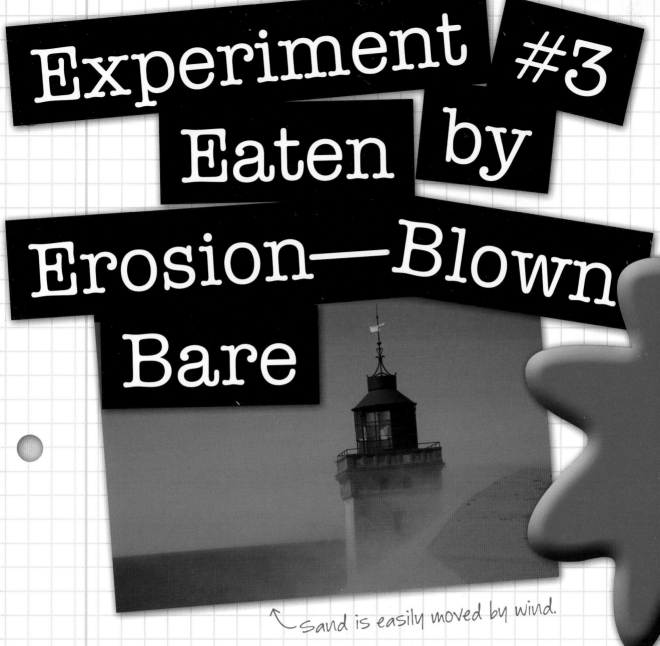

↳ Sand is easily moved by wind.

We now know that weathering has many causes and effects. Do you think the same is true for erosion? Once materials have been broken down into smaller pieces, how are they moved around Earth? One way is by wind. But what makes it easier or more difficult for wind to cause erosion?

Here is one possible hypothesis: **Places with strong winds and exposed soil will erode faster than places with strong winds and better-protected soil.**

Here's what you'll need:
- 2 large sheets of white paper (newspaper will work)
- A flat, clean place outside, such as a sidewalk
- Equal amounts of soil, sand, and gravel (or hot chocolate mix, cornmeal, and dried beans) mixed together
- Objects of various shapes and sizes (bricks, cans, blocks, sticks, rocks, and even small potted plants)
- Balloon
- Ruler

Gather all of your materials before you begin.

Instructions:
1. Lay the 2 sheets of paper on your flat surface, with a little space between them.
2. Spread half of your soil mixture in an even layer on one piece of paper and the other half on the other piece of paper.

3. Set several of your different-sized objects on top of the mixture on one sheet. Leave the other sheet with just the bare mixture.

4. Blow into the balloon to inflate it. Pinch the neck of the balloon closed with your fingers so air doesn't escape.

5. Bend down so the balloon is about 6 inches (15.2 centimeters) from the mixture on the paper with no objects. Use the ruler to make sure you are holding the balloon the correct distance from the paper.

6. Point the neck of the balloon across and slightly down toward the paper. Hold the balloon in one hand, and loosen your grip on the balloon's neck slightly with your other hand to let the air out of the balloon. Don't let the balloon blow away while you do this. What happens to the mixture as the air escapes?

The ruler will help you make sure you use the same distance each time.

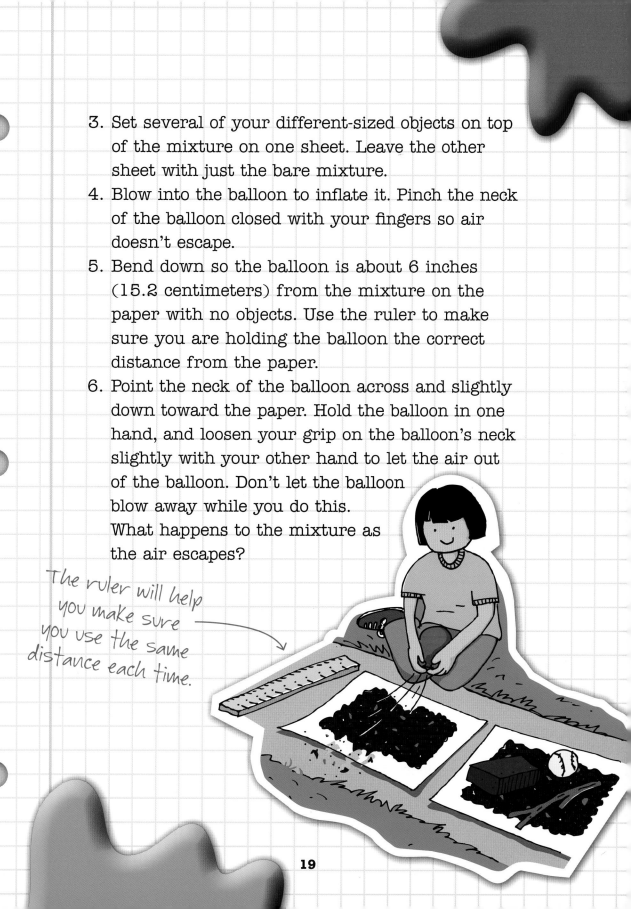

In the 1930s, a drought hit some parts of the United States. It killed plants and crops and dried out the soil. There were no roots to hold the soil in place or water to weigh it down. This made it much easier for winds to sweep the soil away. In 1934 alone, wind was responsible for moving 350 million tons of soil from the western United States all the way to the Atlantic Coast!

7. Inflate the balloon again, and repeat the process with the mixture on the paper that has objects on it. Do some things move? Are some things left behind? Record your observations.

Conclusion:

The air from the balloon represents wind blowing across a landscape. How were the results different for each setup? Did the objects prevent some of the material from being blown away? Was your hypothesis correct? Bare soil can erode faster because there is little to keep it in place. Trees and plants have roots that help anchor the soil. Plants may also act as a physical barrier that helps slow the wind.

Experiment #4
Pushed Ahead, Left Behind

Glaciers are huge chunks of ice.

The soil in the midwestern United States is very fertile. Would you believe this soil was once on land in Canada? What force could have first eroded and then moved all that soil?

Glaciers are masses of ice that are very thick and large. Thousands of years ago, many areas were covered by these slow-moving rivers of ice.

Some glaciers traveled south from Canada into parts of the United States. Could glaciers have something to do with the movement of earthy material? Here is one possible hypothesis: **Glaciers can push ahead or carry along materials such as soil and rock and leave them in another location.**

Here's what you'll need:

- A thin object, such as a book
- Modeling clay
- Baking sheet
- 2 small bowls
- Ice cubes
- Soil
- Sand

You can find modeling clay at a craft store.

Instructions:

1. Flatten the clay into a thin layer across the baking sheet. Leave a strip of bare space at one end of the baking sheet.
2. Use your book or other object to prop up the end of the baking sheet, so the sheet is slightly raised at an angle.

3. Sprinkle some of the soil and sand on top of the clay in a very thin layer.
4. Put a bit of leftover sand in 1 bowl.
5. Place an ice cube on top of the sand in the bowl. Leave it there until some of the sand sticks to the cube.
6. Pick up the ice cube and rub it, sandy side down, on the clay at the top of the baking sheet. Observe how this affects the clay underneath it.
7. Release the ice cube and let it slide down the length of the sheet. What happens to the soil and sand that the ice passes over? Let the ice cube travel all the way down the sheet, until it stops in the bare space. What do you notice about the ice cube? Record your observations.
8. Place the ice cube in the second bowl, and let it melt completely. Examine the water it leaves behind.

What happens to the soil and ice cube? Write it down!

Conclusion:

What did rubbing the sandy ice cube do to the clay? Did anything move with the ice cube when it flowed down the sheet? Was there anything in the water when the ice cube melted? Think of the ice cube as a mini-glacier. A real glacier is much heavier. It can move much larger objects and scrape much deeper into Earth's surface than an ice cube on clay. In nature, the results have been dramatic. Some glaciers have even dug out areas that became lakes. If a glacier melts, deposition may occur. Deposition is the leaving behind of materials in one location that a glacier has pushed, dragged, or picked up from another location. Does this help explain your results? Was your hypothesis correct?

Deposition happens everywhere, even deep underground in caves. Some of the gases present in water can form substances that dissolve rock. That rock is then carried along with the water, until it drips from a cave ceiling and evaporates. Over time, this process deposits enough rock to create amazing formations. They hang down from the ceiling or grow up from the floor in caves.

Experiment #5

Eaten by Erosion— Steep Slopes

↖ A sign warns of the danger of landslides.

If you've ever seen a landslide on television, you might have noticed a lot of soil or rock matter rushing down a slope. Heavy rains can trigger some types of landslides. Do you think the steepness of a slope also affects a landslide? Let's find out.

Come up with a hypothesis that deals with slopes and their effect on soil erosion. Here are two options:

Hypothesis #1: The steeper the slope of a hill, the easier it will be for water to move soil and rocks down that slope.

Hypothesis #2: The steepness of the slope of a hill will have no effect on how easy it is for water to move soil and rocks down that slope.

Here's what you'll need:

- Masking tape
- Paper cup with holes punched in the bottom
- 2 half-gallon (1.9 L) milk cartons
- Scissors
- 2 baking sheets
- 2 cups each of soil, sand, and gravel (or hot chocolate mix, cornmeal, and dried beans) mixed together
- 4 toy blocks
- Drinking glass
- Water

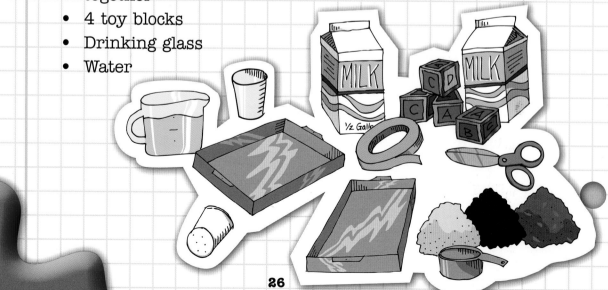

Instructions:

1. Use tape to seal closed the pouring spout of the milk cartons.
2. Use the scissors to cut away an entire side panel of 1 carton. Cut out the bottom, too. Do the same with the other carton.
3. Lay one carton on each baking sheet. The section where you cut away the side panel should be facing up.
4. Divide your soil mixture into 2 equal piles. Put 1 pile in each carton. Make sure the mixture doesn't fall out where you cut away the bottom of the carton.
5. Prop up the spout end of 1 carton with 1 block. Prop up the same end of the other carton using 3 stacked blocks.
6. Fill the drinking glass with water.
7. Hold the paper cup over the raised end of the carton that is propped up with 1 block. Pour the water from the drinking glass into the paper cup. Water should trickle through the paper cup into the mixture. Watch what happens to the mixture as all the water drains. Observe the color of the water as it drains from your carton onto the sheet.
8. Test the other carton in the same way. Sprinkle an equal amount of water over the raised end of the steeper carton. Write down your observations.

Earthquakes, construction activities, or an increase in water content of the soil can affect the stability of materials on a hillside. When that happens, the balance between gravity—which is always pulling down on objects—and the ability of those materials to resist its force is broken. This can cause huge events such as rock slides, a type of erosion called mass wasting. Mass wasting is the movement of earthy matter and rock caused by gravity.

Conclusion:

What happened to the mixture when you poured water over the first carton? Did anything move? What color was the water that drained away? Were your results different for the carton that was raised at a steeper slope? Was more of the mixture carried away? What does this tell us about erosion? You might have noticed that the water flowed more quickly down the steeper slope. Water that moves faster has more energy than slow-moving water. It moves more material. Does this explain your findings? Was your hypothesis correct?

Experiment #6

Do It Yourself!

Now that you're a scientist, you'll probably come up with all kinds of questions when you look around!

Do you still have questions about slopes and erosion? Can erosion be slowed or stopped? Use the same setup as the last experiment to find out. The "hillsides" in our milk cartons were bare. What if you planted things such as plastic forks (with the tines in the soil mixture) to represent trees? Or bits of leaves and small pieces of sponge for bushes and shrubs? Would this reduce erosion caused by water? Come up with a hypothesis to test. Then prepare your materials, write down your instructions, and run the experiment to find out!

Okay, scientists! You now know many new things about erosion. You even learned how to come up with your own hypothesis and test it. Isn't it fun to find answers with experiments?

GLOSSARY

biological weathering (bye-oh-LOJ-i-kuhl WETH-ur-ing) the wearing down of rocks and minerals caused by plants and animals

chemical weathering (KEM-uh-kuhl WETH-ur-ing) the wearing down of rocks and minerals due to changes in their chemical makeup

conclusion (kuhn-KLOO-zhuhn) a final decision, thought, or opinion

erosion (i-ROE-zhuhn) a gradual eating or wearing away by wind, water, or glaciers

hypothesis (hy-POTH-uh-sihss) a logical guess about what will happen in an experiment

mechanical weathering (muh-KAN-uh-kuhl WETH-ur-ing) the breakdown of rocks or other materials through physical means, such as water freezing in a crack in a rock, and not through a chemical change

method (METH-uhd) a way of doing something

observations (ob-zur-VAY-shuhnz) things that are seen or noticed with one's senses

FOR MORE INFORMATION

BOOKS

Bailey, Jacqui. *Cracking Up: A Story about Erosion*. Minneapolis: Picture Window Books, 2006.

Riley, Joelle. *Erosion*. Minneapolis: Lerner Publications, 2007.

Sepehri, Sandy. *Glaciers*. Vero Beach, FL: Rourke Publishing, 2008.

WEB SITES

BBC—Science: Chemistry: Physical Weathering
www.bbc.co.uk/schools/ks3bitesize/science/chemistry/rock_cycle_2.shtml
Find a brief clip showing how water can break rock apart as it freezes and thaws

National Geographic Kids—Earth Movers
magma.nationalgeographic.com/ngexplorer/0610/articles/mainarticle.html
For more information about weathering and erosion

INDEX

About the Authors

Ariel Kazunas is a writer who has worked for several nonprofit magazines. A graduate of Lewis and Clark College, she lives in Portland, Oregon, where she tends to her vegetable garden—and appreciates everything that goes into creating and protecting the soil in which it grows! This is her second book for young readers.

Charnan Simon is a former editor of *Cricket* magazine and the author of more than 100 books for young readers. She lives in Seattle, Washington, where water plays a big part in erosion.